This Gratitude Journal Belongs To:

_____

_____

My Star Rating For Today

Today's Top 3 Best Moments

1.

2.

3.

Today I Am Grateful For...

The Most Awesome Thing
That Happened Today Was...

My Thoughts...

My Doodles...

My Star Rating For Today

Today's Top 3 Best Moments

1.

2.

3.

Today I Am Grateful For...

The Most Awesome Thing
That Happened Today Was...

My Thoughts...

My Doodles...

My Star Rating For Today

Today's Top 3 Best Moments

1.

2.

3.

Today I Am Grateful For...

The Most Awesome Thing
That Happened Today Was...

My Thoughts...

My Doodles...

My Star Rating For Today

Today's Top 3 Best Moments

1.

2.

3.

Today I Am Grateful For...

The Most Awesome Thing
That Happened Today Was...

My Thoughts...

My Doodles...

My Star Rating For Today

Today's Top 3 Best Moments

1.

2.

3.

Today I Am Grateful For...

The Most Awesome Thing
That Happened Today Was...

My Thoughts...

My Doodles...

My Star Rating For Today

Today's Top 3 Best Moments

1.

2.

3.

Today I Am Grateful For...

The Most Awesome Thing
That Happened Today Was...

My Thoughts...

My Doodles...

My Star Rating For Today

Today's Top 3 Best Moments

1.

2.

3.

Today I Am Grateful For...

The Most Awesome Thing That Happened Today Was...

My Thoughts...

My Doodles...

My Star Rating For Today

Today's Top 3 Best Moments

1.

2.

3.

Today I Am Grateful For...

The Most Awesome Thing
That Happened Today Was...

My Thoughts...

My Doodles...

My Star Rating For Today

Today's Top 3 Best Moments

1.

2.

3.

Today I Am Grateful For...

The Most Awesome Thing
That Happened Today Was...

My Thoughts...

My Doodles...

My Star Rating For Today

Today's Top 3 Best Moments

1.

2.

3.

Today I Am Grateful For...

The Most Awesome Thing
That Happened Today Was...

My Thoughts...

My Doodles...

My Star Rating For Today

Today's Top 3 Best Moments

1.

2.

3.

Today I Am Grateful For...

The Most Awesome Thing That Happened Today Was...

My Thoughts...

My Doodles...

My Star Rating For Today

Today's Top 3 Best Moments

1.

2.

3.

Today I Am Grateful For...

The Most Awesome Thing That Happened Today Was...

My Thoughts...

My Doodles...

My Star Rating For Today

Today's Top 3 Best Moments

1.

2.

3.

Today I Am Grateful For...

The Most Awesome Thing That Happened Today Was...

My Thoughts...

My Doodles...

My Star Rating For Today

Today's Top 3 Best Moments

1.

2.

3.

Today I Am Grateful For...

The Most Awesome Thing That Happened Today Was...

My Thoughts...

My Doodles...

My Star Rating For Today

Today's Top 3 Best Moments

1.

2.

3.

Today I Am Grateful For...

The Most Awesome Thing
That Happened Today Was...

My Thoughts...

My Doodles...

My Star Rating For Today

Today's Top 3 Best Moments

1.

2.

3.

Today I Am Grateful For...

The Most Awesome Thing
That Happened Today Was...

My Thoughts...

My Doodles...

My Star Rating For Today

Today's Top 3 Best Moments

1.

2.

3.

Today I Am Grateful For...

The Most Awesome Thing That Happened Today Was...

My Thoughts...

My Doodles...

My Star Rating For Today

Today's Top 3 Best Moments

1.

2.

3.

Today I Am Grateful For...

The Most Awesome Thing
That Happened Today Was...

My Thoughts...

My Doodles...

My Star Rating For Today

Today's Top 3 Best Moments

1.

2.

3.

Today I Am Grateful For...

The Most Awesome Thing
That Happened Today Was...

My Thoughts...

My Doodles...

My Star Rating For Today

Today's Top 3 Best Moments

1.

2.

3.

Today I Am Grateful For...

The Most Awesome Thing
That Happened Today Was...

My Thoughts...

My Doodles...

My Star Rating For Today

Today's Top 3 Best Moments

1.

2.

3.

Today I Am Grateful For...

The Most Awesome Thing
That Happened Today Was...

My Thoughts...

My Doodles...

My Star Rating For Today

Today's Top 3 Best Moments

1.

2.

3.

Today I Am Grateful For...

The Most Awesome Thing That Happened Today Was...

My Thoughts...

My Doodles...

My Star Rating For Today

Today's Top 3 Best Moments

1.

2.

3.

Today I Am Grateful For...

The Most Awesome Thing
That Happened Today Was...

My Thoughts...

My Doodles...

My Star Rating For Today

Today's Top 3 Best Moments

1.

2.

3.

Today I Am Grateful For...

The Most Awesome Thing
That Happened Today Was...

My Thoughts...

My Doodles...

My Star Rating For Today

Today's Top 3 Best Moments

1.

2.

3.

Today I Am Grateful For...

The Most Awesome Thing
That Happened Today Was...

My Thoughts...

My Doodles...

My Star Rating For Today

Today's Top 3 Best Moments

1.

2.

3.

Today I Am Grateful For...

The Most Awesome Thing That Happened Today Was...

My Thoughts...

My Doodles...

My Star Rating For Today

Today's Top 3 Best Moments

1.

2.

3.

Today I Am Grateful For...

The Most Awesome Thing
That Happened Today Was...

My Thoughts...

My Doodles...

My Star Rating For Today

Today's Top 3 Best Moments

1.

2.

3.

Today I Am Grateful For...

The Most Awesome Thing
That Happened Today Was...

My Thoughts...

My Doodles...

My Star Rating For Today

Today's Top 3 Best Moments

1.

2.

3.

Today I Am Grateful For...

The Most Awesome Thing
That Happened Today Was...

My Thoughts...

My Doodles...

My Star Rating For Today

Today's Top 3 Best Moments

1.

2.

3.

Today I Am Grateful For...

The Most Awesome Thing
That Happened Today Was...

My Thoughts...

My Doodles...

CPSIA information can be obtained
at www.ICGtesting.com
Printed in the USA
LVHW021223221219
641386LV00012B/2842/P